PENGUIN BOO...

Elegy Written i...

and...

ELEGY
WRITTEN
IN A
COUNTRY
CHURCHYARD

and other
poems

Selected by SIMON WINDER

English Journeys

PENGUIN BOOKS

Published by the Penguin Group
Penguin Books Ltd, 80 Strand, London WC2R ORL, England
Penguin Group (USA) Inc., 375 Hudson Street, New York, New York 10014, USA
Penguin Group (Canada), 90 Eglinton Avenue East, Suite 700, Toronto, Ontario, Canada M4P 2Y3
(a division of Pearson Penguin Canada Inc.)
Penguin Ireland, 25 St Stephen's Green, Dublin 2, Ireland
(a division of Penguin Books Ltd)
Penguin Group (Australia), 250 Camberwell Road, Camberwell, Victoria 3124, Australia
(a division of Pearson Australia Group Pty Ltd)
Penguin Books India Pvt Ltd, 11 Community Centre, Panchsheel Park, New Delhi – 110 017, India
Penguin Group (NZ), 67 Apollo Drive, Rosedale, North Shore 0632, New Zealand
(a division of Pearson New Zealand Ltd)
Penguin Books (South Africa) (Pty) Ltd, 24 Sturdee Avenue, Rosebank, Johannesburg 2196, South Africa

Penguin Books Ltd, Registered Offices: 80 Strand, London WC2R ORL, England

www.penguin.com

This selection published in Penguin Books 2009

3

Set by Rowland Phototypesetting Ltd, Bury St Edmunds, Suffolk
Printed in England by Clays Ltd, St Ives plc

978-0-141-19083-9

www.greenpenguin.co.uk

Penguin Books is committed to a sustainable future
for our business, our readers and our planet.
The book in your hands is made from paper
certified by the Forest Stewardship Council.

Contents

Edward Thomas (1878–1917)

Charles Cotton Evening Quatrains

The Day's grown old, the fainting Sun
Has but a little way to run,
And yet his Steeds, with all his skill,
Scarce lug the Chariot down the Hill.

With Labour spent, and Thirst opprest,
Whilst they strain hard to gain the West,
From Fetlocks hot drops melted light,
Which turn to Meteors in the Night.

The Shadows now so long do grow,
That Brambles like tall Cedars show,
Mole-hills seem Mountains, and the Ant
Appears a monstrous Elephant.

A very little little Flock
Shades thrice the ground that it would stock;
Whilst the small Stripling following them,
Appears a mighty *Polypheme*.

These being brought into the Fold,
And by the thrifty Master told,
He thinks his Wages are well paid,
Since none are either lost, or stray'd.

Now lowing Herds are each-where heard,
Chains rattle in the Villains Yard,
The Cart's on Tayl set down to rest,
Bearing on high the Cuckolds Crest.

The hedg is stript, the Clothes brought in,
Nought's left without should be within,
The Bees are hiv'd, and hum their Charm,
Whilst every House does seem a Swarm.

The Cock now to the Roost is prest:
For he must call up all the rest;
The Sow's fast pegg'd within the Sty,
To still her squeaking Progeny.

Each one has had his Supping Mess,
The Cheese is put into the Press,
The Pans and Bowls clean scalded all,
Rear'd up against the Milk-house Wall.

And now on Benches all are sat
In the cool Air to sit and chat,
Till *Phœbus*, dipping in the West,
Shall lead the World the way to Rest.

To My Dear and Most Worthy Friend, Mr. Isaak Walton

Whilst in this cold and blust'ring Clime,
    Where bleak winds howl, and Tempests roar,
We pass away the roughest time
    Has been of many years before;

Whilst from the most tempest'ous Nooks
    The chillest Blasts our peace invade,
And by great Rains our smallest Brooks
    Are almost navigable made;

Whilst all the ills are so improv'd
    Of this dead quarter of the year,
That even you, so much belov'd,
    We would not now wish with us here;

In this estate, I say, it is
    Some comfort to us to suppose,
That in a better Clime than this
    You our dear Friend have more repose;

And some delight to me the while,
    Though nature now does weep in Rain,
To think that I have seen her smile,
    And haply may I do again.

If the all-ruling Power please
      We live to see another *May*,
We'll recompence an Age of these
      Foul days in one fine fishing day:

We then shall have a day or two,
      Perhaps a week, wherein to try,
What the best Master's hand can doe
      With the most deadly killing Flie:

A day without too bright a Beam,
      A warm, but not a scorching Sun,
A Southern gale to curl the Stream,
      And (Master) half our work is done.

There whilst behind some bush we wait
      The Scaly People to betray,
We'll prove it just with treach'rous Bait
      To make the preying Trout our prey;

And think our selves in such an hour
      Happier than those, though not so high,
Who, like Leviathans, devour
      Of meaner men the smaller Fry.

This (my best Friend) at my poor Home
      Shall be our Pastime and our Theme,
But then should you not deign to come
      You make all this a flatt'ring Dream.

Alexander Pope *Windsor Forest*

Thy forests, Windsor! and thy green retreats,
At once the monarch's and the muse's seats,
Invite my lays. Be present, sylvan maids!
Unlock your springs, and open all your shades.
GRANVILLE commands; your aid, O muses, bring!
What muse for GRANVILLE can refuse to sing?
     The groves of Eden, vanished now so long,
Live in description, and look green in song:
These, were my breast inspired with equal flame,
Like them in beauty, should be like in fame.
Here hills and vales, the woodland and the plain,
Here earth and water seem to strive again,
Not chaos-like together crushed and bruised,
But, as the world, harmoniously confused:
Where order in variety we see,
And where, though all things differ, all agree.
Here waving groves a chequered scene display,
And part admit, and part exclude the day;
As some coy nymph her lover's warm address
Nor quite indulges, nor can quite repress.
There, interspersed in lawns and opening glades,
Thin trees arise that shun each other's shades.
Here in full light the russet plains extend:
There wrapped in clouds the blueish hills ascend.
Ev'n the wild heath displays her purple dyes,

And 'midst the desert fruitful fields arise,
That crowned with tufted trees and springing corn,
Like verdant isles the sable waste adorn.
Let India boast her plants, nor envy we
The weeping amber or the balmy tree,
While by our oaks the precious loads are born,
And realms commanded which those trees adorn.
Not proud Olympus yields a nobler sight,
Though Gods assembled grace his towering height,
Than what more humble mountains offer here,
Where, in their blessings, all those Gods appear.
See Pan with flocks, with fruits Pomona crowned,
Here blushing Flora paints th'enamelled ground,
Here Ceres' gifts in waving prospect stand,
And nodding tempt the joyful reaper's hand;
Rich Industry sits smiling on the plains,
And peace and plenty tell, a STUART reigns.

　　Not thus the land appeared in ages past,
A dreary desert, and a gloomy waste,
To savage beasts and savage laws a prey,
And kings more furious and severe than they;
Who claimed the skies, dispeopled air and floods,
The lonely lords of empty wilds and woods:
Cities laid waste, they stormed the dens and caves,
(For wiser brutes were backward to be slaves.)
What could be free, when lawless beasts obeyed,
And ev'n the elements a tyrant swayed?
In vain kind seasons swelled the teeming grain,
Soft showers distilled, and suns grew warm in vain;
The swain with tears his frustrate labour yields,
And famished dies amidst his ripened fields.

What wonder then, a beast or subject slain
Were equal crimes in a despotic reign?
Both doomed alike, for sportive tyrants bled,
But while the subject starved, the beast was fed.
Proud Nimrod first the bloody chase began,
A mighty hunter, and his prey was man:
Our haughty Norman boasts that barbarous
        name,
And makes his trembling slaves the royal game.
The fields are ravished from th'industrious swains,
From men their cities, and from Gods their fanes:
The levelled towns with weeds lie covered o'er;
The hollow winds through naked temples roar;
Round broken columns clasping ivy twined;
O'er heaps of ruin stalked the stately hind;
The fox obscene to gaping tombs retires,
And savage howlings fill the sacred quires.
Awed by his nobles, by his commons cursed,
Th'oppressor ruled tyrannic where he durst,
Stretched o'er the poor and church his iron rod,
And served alike his vassals and his God.
Whom ev'n the Saxon spared and bloody Dane,
The wanton victims of his sport remain.
But see, the man who spacious regions gave
A waste for beasts, himself denied a grave!
Stretched on the lawn his second hope survey,
At once the chaser, and at once the prey:
Lo Rufus, tugging at the deadly dart,
Bleeds in the forest, like a wounded hart.
Succeeding monarchs heard the subjects' cries,
Nor saw displeased the peaceful cottage rise.

Then gathering flocks on unknown mountains fed,
O'er sandy wilds were yellow harvests spread,
The forests wondered at th' unusual grain,
And secret transport touched the conscious swain.
Fair Liberty, Britannia's Goddess, rears
Her cheerful head, and leads the golden years.

   Ye vigorous swains! while youth ferments your
      blood,
And purer spirits swell the sprightly flood,
Now range the hills, the gameful woods beset,
Wind the shrill horn, or spread the waving net.
When milder autumn summer's heat succeeds,
And in the new-shorn field the partridge feeds,
Before his lord the ready spaniel bounds,
Panting with hope, he tries the furrowed grounds;
But when the tainted gales the game betray,
Couched close he lies, and meditates the prey:
Secure they trust th' unfaithful field, beset,
Till hovering o'er 'em sweeps the swelling net.
Thus (if small things we may with great compare)
When Albion sends her eager sons to war,
Some thoughtless town, with ease and plenty
      blessed,
Near, and more near, the closing lines invest;
Sudden they seize th' amazed, defenceless prize,
And high in air Britannia's standard flies.

   See! from the brake the whirring pheasant
      springs,
And mounts exulting on triumphant wings:
Short is his joy; he feels the fiery wound,
Flutters in blood, and panting beats the ground.

Ah! what avail his glossy, varying dyes,
His purple crest, and scarlet-circled eyes,
The vivid green his shining plumes unfold,
His painted wings, and breast that flames with
      gold?
  Nor yet, when moist Arcturus clouds the sky,
The woods and fields their pleasing toils deny.
To plains with well-breathed beagles we repair,
And trace the mazes of the circling hare:
(Beasts, urged by us, their fellow-beasts pursue,
And learn of man each other to undo.)
With slaughtering guns th' unwearied fowler roves,
When frosts have whitened all the naked groves;
Where doves in flocks the leafless trees o'ershade,
And lonely woodcocks haunt the watery glade.
He lifts the tube, and levels with his eye;
Straight a short thunder breaks the frozen sky.
Oft, as in airy rings they skim the heath,
The clamorous lapwings feel the leaden death:
Oft, as the mounting larks their notes prepare,
They fall, and leave their little lives in air.
  In genial spring, beneath the quivering shade,
Where cooling vapours breathe along the mead,
The patient fisher takes his silent stand,
Intent, his angle trembling in his hand;
With looks unmoved, he hopes the scaly breed,
And eyes the dancing cork, and bending reed.
Our plenteous streams a various race supply,
The bright-eyed perch with fins of Tyrian dye,
The silver eel, in shining volumes rolled,
The yellow carp, in scales bedropped with gold,

Swift trouts, diversified with crimson stains,
And pikes, the tyrants of the watery plains.
  Now Cancer glows with Phoebus' fiery car:
The youth rush eager to the sylvan war,
Swarm o'er the lawns, the forest walks surround,
Rouse the fleet hart, and cheer the opening hound.
Th' impatient courser pants in every vein,
And pawing, seems to beat the distant plain:
Hills, vales, and floods appear already crossed,
And e'er he starts, a thousand steps are lost.
See the bold youth strain up the threatening steep,
Rush through the thickets, down the valleys
      sweep,
Hang o'er their coursers heads with eager speed,
And earth rolls back beneath the flying steed.
Let old Arcadia boast her ample plain,
Th' immortal huntress, and her virgin-train;
Nor envy, Windsor! since thy shades have seen
As bright a Goddess, and as chaste a QUEEN;
Whose care, like hers, protects the sylvan reign,
The earth's fair light, and empress of the main.
  Here too, 'tis sung, of old Diana strayed,
And Cynthus' top forsook for Windsor shade;
Here was she seen o'er airy wastes to rove,
Seek the clear spring, or haunt the pathless grove;
Here armed with silver bows, in early dawn,
Her buskined virgins traced the dewy lawn.
  Above the rest a rural nymph was famed,
Thy offspring, Thames! the fair Lodona named;
(Lodona's fate, in long oblivion cast,
The Muse shall sing, and what she sings shall last.)

Scarce could the Goddess from her nymph be
        known,
But by the crescent and the golden zone:
She scorned the praise of beauty, and the care;
A belt her waist, a fillet binds her hair;
A painted quiver on her shoulder sounds,
And with her dart the flying deer she wounds.
It chanced, as eager of the chase the maid
Beyond the forest's verdant limits strayed,
Pan saw and loved, and burning with desire
Pursued her flight, her flight increased his fire.
Not half so swift the trembling doves can fly,
When the fierce eagle cleaves the liquid sky;
Not half so swiftly the fierce eagle moves,
When through the clouds he drives the trembling
        doves;
As from the God she flew with furious pace,
Or as the God, more furious, urged the chase.
Now fainting, sinking, pale, the nymph appears;
Now close behind his sounding steps she hears;
And now his shadow reached her as she run,
(His shadow lengthened by the setting sun)
And now his shorter breath, with sultry air,
Pants on her neck, and fans her parting hair.
In vain on Father Thames she calls for aid,
Nor could Diana help her injured maid.
Faint, breathless, thus she prayed, nor prayed in vain;
'Ah Cynthia! ah – though banished from thy
        train,
Let me, O let me, to the shades repair,
My native shades – there weep, and murmur there.'

She said, and melting as in tears she lay,
In a soft, silver stream dissolved away.
The silver stream her virgin coldness keeps,
For ever murmurs, and for ever weeps;
She still bears the name the hapless virgin bore,
And bathes the forest where she ranged before.
In her chaste current oft the Goddess laves,
And with celestial tears augments the waves.
Oft in her glass the musing shepherd spies
The headlong mountains and the downward skies.
The watery landskip of the pendant woods,
And absent trees that tremble in the floods;
In the clear azure gleam the flocks are seen,
And floating forests paint the waves with green.
Through the fair scene roll slow the lingering
        streams,
Then foaming pour along, and rush into the Thames.
    Thou too, great father of the British floods!
With joyful pride surveyst our lofty woods;
Where towering oaks their growing honours rear,
And future navies on thy shores appear.
Not Neptune's self from all her streams receives
A wealthier tribute, than to thine he gives.
No seas so rich, so gay no banks appear,
No lake so gentle, and no spring so clear.
Nor Po so swells the fabling poet's lays,
While led along the skies his current strays,
As thine, which visits Windsor's famed abodes,
To grace the mansion of our earthly Gods:
Nor all his stars above a lustre show,
Like the bright beauties on thy banks below;

Where Jove, subdued by mortal passion still,
Might change Olympus for a nobler hill.
   Happy the man whom this bright court
      approves,
His sovereign favours, and his country loves:
Happy next him, who to these shades retires,
Whom nature charms, and whom the Muse
      inspires:
Whom humbler joys of home-felt quiet please,
Successive study, exercise, and ease.
He gathers health from herbs the forest yields,
And of their fragrant physic spoils the fields:
With chymic art exalts the mineral powers,
And draws the aromatic souls of flowers:
Now marks the course of rolling orbs on high;
O'er figured worlds now travels with his eye;
Of ancient writ unlocks the learned store,
Consults the dead, and lives past ages o'er:
Or wandering thoughtful in the silent wood,
Attends the duties of the wise and good,
T'observe a mean, be to himself a friend,
To follow nature, and regard his end;
Or looks on heaven with more than mortal eyes,
Bids his free soul expatiate in the skies,
Amid her kindred stars familiar roam,
Survey the region, and confess her home!
Such was the life great Scipio once admired,
Thus Atticus, and TRUMBULL thus retired.
   Ye sacred Nine! that all my soul possess,
Whose raptures fire me, and whole visions
      bless,

Bear me, oh bear me to sequestered scenes,
The bowery mazes, and surrounding greens:
To Thames's banks which fragrant breezes fill,
Or where ye Muses sport on COOPER'S HILL.
(On COOPER'S HILL eternal wreaths shall grow,
While lasts the mountain, or while Thames shall
    flow)
I seem through consecrated walks to rove,
I hear soft music die along the grove:
Led by the sound, I roam from shade to shade,
By god-like poets venerable made:
Here his first lays majestic DENHAM sung;
There the last numbers flowed from COWLEY'S
    tongue.
O early lost! what tears the river shed,
When the sad pomp along his banks was led?
His drooping swans on every note expire,
And on his willows hung each Muse's lyre.
  Since fate relentless stopped their heavenly voice,
No more the forests ring, or groves rejoice;
Who now shall charm the shades, where COWLEY
    strung
His living harp, and lofty DENHAM sung?
But hark! the groves rejoice, the forest rings!
Are these revived? or is it GRANVILLE sings?
'Tis yours, my lord, to bless our soft retreats,
And call the Muses to their ancient seats;
To paint anew the flowery sylvan scenes,
To crown the forests with immortal greens,
Make Windsor hills in lofty numbers rise,
And lift her turrets nearer to the skies;

To sing those honours you deserve to wear,
And add new lustre to her silver star.
   Here noble SURREY felt the sacred rage,
SURREY, the GRANVILLE of a former age:
Matchless his pen, victorious was his lance,
Bold in the lists, and graceful in the dance:
In the same shades the Cupids tuned his lyre,
To the same notes, of love, and soft desire:
Fair Geraldine, bright object of his vow,
Then filled the groves, as heavenly Myra now.
      Oh wouldst thou sing what heroes Windsor
         bore,
What kings first breathed upon her winding
         shore,
Or raise old warriors, whose adored remains
In weeping vaults her hallowed earth contains!
With Edward's acts adorn the shining page,
Stretch his long triumphs down through every age,
Draw monarchs chained, and Cressi's glorious
         field,
The lilies blazing on the regal shield:
Then, from her roofs when Verrio's colours fall,
And leave inanimate the naked wall,
Still in thy song should vanquished France appear,
And bleed for ever under Britain's spear.
   Let softer strains ill-fated Henry mourn,
And palms eternal flourish round his urn.
Here o'er the Martyr-King the marble weeps,
And fast beside him, once-feared Edward sleeps:
Whom not th' extended Albion could contain,
From old Belerium to the northern main,

The grave unites; where ev'n the great find rest,
And blended lie th' oppressor and th' oppressed!
  Make sacred Charles's tomb for ever known,
(Obscure the place, and un-inscribed the stone)
Oh fact accursed! what tears has Albion shed,
Heavens, what new wounds! and how her old have
        bled?
She saw her sons with purple deaths expire,
Her sacred domes involved in rolling fire,
A dreadful series of intestine wars,
Inglorious triumphs and dishonest scars,
At length great ANNA said – 'Let Discord cease!'
She said, the world obeyed, and all was peace!
  In that blessed moment from his oozy bed
Old Father Thames advanced his reverend head.
His tresses dropped with dews, and o'er the stream
His shining horns diffused a golden gleam:
Graved on his urn appeared the moon, that guides
His swelling waters, and alternate tides;
The figured streams in waves of silver rolled,
And on their banks Augusta rose in gold.
Around his throne the sea-born brothers stood,
Who swell with tributary urns his flood;
First the famed authors of his ancient name,
The winding Isis and the fruitful Thame:
The Kennet swift, for silver eels renowned;
The Loddon slow, with verdant alders crowned;
Cole, whose dark streams his flowery islands lave;
And chalky Wey, that rolls a milky wave:
The blue, transparent Vandalis appears;
The gulphy Lea his sedgy tresses rears;

And sullen Mole, that hides his diving flood;
And silent Darent, stained with Danish blood.

   High in the midst, upon his urn reclined,
(His sea-green mantle waving with the wind)
The God appeared: he turned his azure eyes
Where Windsor domes and pompous turrets rise;
Then bowed and spoke; the winds forget to roar,
And the hushed waves glide softly to the shore.

   Hail, sacred Peace! hail long-expected days,
That Thames's glory to the stars shall raise!
Though Tiber's streams immortal Rome behold,
Though foaming Hermus swells with tides of gold,
From heaven itself though seven-fold Nilus flows,
And harvests on a hundred realms bestows;
These now no more shall be the Muse's themes,
Lost in my fame, as in the sea their streams.
Let Volga's banks with iron squadrons shine,
And groves of lances glitter on the Rhine,
Let barbarous Ganges arm a servile train;
Be mine the blessings of a peaceful reign.
No more my sons shall dye with British blood
Red Iber's sands, or Ister's foaming flood:
Safe on my shore each unmolested swain
Shall tend the flocks, or reap the bearded grain;
The shady empire shall retain no trace
Of war or blood, but in the sylvan chase;
The trumpets sleep, while cheerful horns are
      blown,
And arms employed on birds and beasts alone.
Behold! th' ascending villas on my side,
Project long shadows o'er the crystal tide.

Behold! Augusta's glittering spires increase,
And temples rise, the beauteous works of peace.
I see, I see where two fair cities bend
Their ample bow, a new Whitehall ascend!
There mighty nations shall enquire their doom,
The world's great oracle in times to come;
There kings shall sue, and suppliant states be seen
Once more to bend before a BRITISH QUEEN.

    Thy trees, fair Windsor! now shall leave their
        woods,
And half thy forests rush into my floods,
Bear Britain's thunder, and her cross display,
To the bright regions of the rising day;
Tempt icy seas, where scarce the waters roll,
Where clearer flames glow round the frozen pole;
Or under southern skies exalt their sails,
Led by new stars, and borne by spicy gales!
For me the balm shall bleed, and amber flow,
The coral redden, and the ruby glow,
The pearly shell its lucid globe infold,
And Phoebus warm the ripening ore to gold.
The time shall come, when free as seas or wind
Unbounded Thames shall flow for all mankind,
Whole nations enter with each swelling tide,
And seas but join the regions they divide;
Earth's distant ends our glory shall behold,
And the new world launch forth to seek the old.
Then ships of uncouth form shall stem the tide,
And feathered people crowd my wealthy side,
And naked youths and painted chiefs admire
Our speech, our colour, and our strange attire!

Oh stretch thy reign, fair Peace! from shore to
     shore,
Till conquest cease, and slavery be no more;
Till the freed Indians in their native groves
Reap their own fruits, and woo their sable loves,
Peru once more a race of kings behold,
And other Mexicos be roofed with gold.
Exiled by thee from earth to deepest hell,
In brazen bonds shall barbarous Discord dwell;
Gigantic Pride, pale Terror, gloomy Care,
And mad Ambition shall attend her there:
There purple Vengeance bathed in gore retires,
Her weapons blunted, and extinct her fires:
There hateful Envy her own snakes shall feel,
And Persecution mourn her broken wheel:
There Faction roar, Rebellion bite her chain,
And gasping Furies thirst for blood in vain.

   Here cease thy flight, nor with unhallowed lays
Touch the fair fame of Albion's golden days:
The thoughts of Gods let GRANVILLE's verse
     recite,
And bring the scenes of opening fate to light.
My humble Muse, in unambitious strains,
Paints the green forests and the flowery plains,
Where Peace descending bids her olives spring,
And scatters blessings from her dove-like wing.
Ev'n I more sweetly pass my careless days,
Pleased in the silent shade with empty praise;
Enough for me, that to the listening swains
First in these fields I sung the sylvan strains.

James Thomson from Summer

                        The daw,
The rook, and magpie, to the grey-grown oaks
(That the calm village in their verdant arms,
Sheltering, embrace) direct their lazy flight;
Where on the mingling boughs they sit embowered
All the hot noon, till cooler hours arise.
Faint underneath the household fowls convene;
And, in a corner of the buzzing shade,
The house-dog with the vacant greyhound lies
Out-stretched and sleepy. In his slumbers one
Attacks the nightly thief, and one exults
O'er hill and dale; till, wakened by the wasp,
They starting snap. Nor shall the muse disdain
To let the little noisy summer-race
Live in her lay and flutter through her song:
Not mean though simple – to the sun allied,
From him they draw their animating fire.

    Waked by his warmer ray, the reptile young
Come winged abroad, by the light air upborne,
Lighter, and full of soul. From every chink
And secret corner, where they slept away
The wintry storms, or rising from their tombs
To higher life, by myriads forth at once
Swarming they pour, of all the varied hues
Their beauty-beaming parent can disclose.

Ten thousand forms, ten thousand different tribes
People the blaze. To sunny waters some
By fatal instinct fly; where on the pool
They sportive wheel, or, sailing down the stream,
Are snatched immediate by the quick-eyed trout
Or darting salmon. Through the green-wood glade
Some love to stray; there lodged, amused, and fed
In the fresh leaf. Luxurious, others make
The meads their choice, and visit every flower
And every latent herb: for the sweet task
To propagate their kinds, and where to wrap
In what soft beds their young, yet undisclosed,
Employs their tender care. Some to the house,
The fold, and dairy hungry bend their flight;
Sip round the pail, or taste the curdling cheese:
Oft, inadvertent, from the milky stream
They meet their fate; or, weltering in the bowl,
With powerless wings around them wrapt, expire.

(. . .)

Resounds the living surface of the ground:
Nor undelightful is the ceaseless hum
To him who muses through the woods at noon,
Or drowsy shepherd as he lies reclined,
With half-shut eyes, beneath the floating shade
Of willows grey, close-crowding o'er the brook,
   Gradual from these what numerous kinds descend,
Evading even the microscopic eye!
Full Nature swarms with life; one wondrous mass
Of animals, or atoms organized

Waiting the vital breath when Parent-Heaven
Shall bid his spirit blow. The hoary fen
In putrid streams emits the living cloud
Of pestilence. Through subterranean cells,
Where searching sunbeams scarce can find a way,
Earth animated heaves. The flowery leaf
Wants not its soft inhabitants. Secure
Within its winding citadel the stone
Holds multitudes. But chief the forest boughs,
That dance unnumbered to the playful breeze,
The downy orchard, and the melting pulp
Of mellow fruit the nameless nations feed
Of evanescent insects. Where the pool
Stands mantled o'er with green, invisible
Amid the floating verdure millions stray.
Each liquid too, whether it pierces, soothes,
Inflames, refreshes, or exalts the taste,
With various forms abounds. Nor is the stream
Of purest crystal, nor the lucid air,
Though one transparent vacancy it seems,
Void of their unseen people. These, concealed
By the kind art of forming Heaven, escape
The grosser eye of man: for, if the worlds
In worlds inclosed should on his senses burst,
From cates ambrosial and the nectared bowl
He would abhorrent turn; and in dead night,
When Silence sleeps o'er all, be stunned with noise.

Thomas Gray Elegy Written in a Country Churchyard

The Curfew tolls the knell of parting day,
The lowing herd wind slowly o'er the lea,
The plowman homeward plods his weary way,
And leaves the world to darkness and to me.

Now fades the glimmering landscape on the sight,
And all the air a solemn stillness holds,
Save where the beetle wheels his droning flight,
And drowsy tinklings lull the distant folds;

Save that from yonder ivy-mantled tow'r
The mopeing owl does to the moon complain
Of such, as wand'ring near her secret bow'r,
Molest her ancient solitary reign.

Beneath those rugged elms, that yew-tree's shade,
Where heaves the turf in many a mould'ring heap,
Each in his narrow cell for ever laid,
The rude Forefathers of the hamlet sleep.

The breezy call of incense-breathing Morn,
The swallow twitt'ring from the straw-built shed,
The cock's shrill clarion, or the ecchoing horn,
No more shall rouse them from their lowly bed.

For them no more the blazing hearth shall burn,
Or busy housewife ply her evening care:
No children run to lisp their sire's return,
Or climb his knees the envied kiss to share.

Oft did the harvest to their sickle yield,
Their furrow oft the stubborn glebe has broke;
How jocund did they drive their team afield!
How bow'd the woods beneath their sturdy stroke!

Let not Ambition mock their useful toil,
Their homely joys, and destiny obscure;
Nor Grandeur hear with a disdainful smile,
The short and simple annals of the poor.

The boast of heraldry, the pomp of pow'r,
And all that beauty, all that wealth e'er gave,
Awaits alike th' inevitable hour.
The paths of glory lead but to the grave.

Nor you, ye Proud, impute to These the fault,
If Mem'ry o'er their Tomb no Trophies raise,
Where thro' the long-drawn isle and fretted vault
The pealing anthem swells the note of praise.

Can storied urn or animated bust
Back to its mansion call the fleeting breath?
Can Honour's voice provoke the silent dust,
Or Flatt'ry sooth the dull cold ear of Death?

Perhaps in this neglected spot is laid
Some heart once pregnant with celestial fire,
Hands, that the rod of empire might have sway'd,
Or wak'd to extasy the living lyre.

But Knowledge to their eyes her ample page
Rich with the spoils of time did ne'er unroll;
Chill Penury repress'd their noble rage,
And froze the genial current of the soul.

Full many a gem of purest ray serene,
The dark unfathom'd caves of ocean bear:
Full many a flower is born to blush unseen,
And waste its sweetness on the desert air.

Some village-Hampden, that with dauntless breast
The little Tyrant of his fields withstood;
Some mute inglorious Milton here may rest,
Some Cromwell guiltless of his country's blood.

Th' applause of list'ning senates to command,
The threats of pain and ruin to despise,
To scatter plenty o'er a smiling land,
And read their hist'ry in a nation's eyes

Their lot forbad: nor circumscrib'd alone
Their growing virtues, but their crimes confin'd;
Forbad to wade through slaughter to a throne,
And shut the gates of mercy on mankind,

The struggling pangs of conscious truth to hide,
To quench the blushes of ingenuous shame,
Or heap the shrine of Luxury and Pride
With incense kindled at the Muse's flame.

Far from the madding crowd's ignoble strife,
Their sober wishes never learn'd to stray;
Along the cool sequester'd vale of life
They kept the noiseless tenor of their way.

Yet ev'n these bones from insult to protect
Some frail memorial still erected nigh,
With uncouth rhimes and shapeless sculpture
    deck'd,
Implores the passing tribute of a sigh.

Their name, their years, spelt by th' unletter'd
    muse,
The place of fame and elegy supply:
And many a holy text around she strews,
That teach the rustic moralist to die.

For who to dumb Forgetfulness a prey,
This pleasing anxious being e'er resign'd,
Left the warm precincts of the chearful day,
Nor cast one longing ling'ring look behind?

On some fond breast the parting soul relies,
Some pious drops the closing eye requires;
Ev'n from the tomb the voice of Nature cries,
Ev'n in our Ashes live their wonted Fires.

For thee, who mindful of th' unhonour'd Dead
Dost in these lines their artless tale relate;
If chance, by lonely contemplation led,
Some kindred Spirit shall inquire thy fate,

Haply some hoary-headed Swain may say,
'Oft have we seen him at the peep of dawn
'Brushing with hasty steps the dews away
'To meet the sun upon the upland lawn.

'There at the foot of yonder nodding beech
'That wreathes its old fantastic roots so high,
'His listless length at noontide wou'd he stretch,
'And pore upon the brook that babbles by.

'Hard by yon wood, now smiling as in scorn,
'Mutt'ring his wayward fancies he wou'd rove,
'Now drooping, woeful wan, like one forlorn,
'Or craz'd with care, or cross'd in hopeless love.

'One morn I miss'd him on the custom'd hill,
'Along the heath and near his fav'rite tree;
'Another came; nor yet beside the rill,
'Nor up the lawn, nor at the wood was he,

'The next with dirges due in sad array
'Slow thro' the church-way path we saw him
        born[e].
'Approach and read (for thou can'st read) the lay,
'Grav'd on the stone beneath yon aged thorn.'

The Epitaph

Here rests his head upon the lap of Earth
A Youth to Fortune and to Fame unknown,
Fair Science frown'd not on his humble birth,
And Melancholy mark'd him for her own.

Large was his bounty, and his soul sincere,
Heav'n did a recompence as largely send:
He gave to Mis'ry all he had, a tear,
He gain'd from Heav'n ('twas all he wish'd) a friend.

No farther seek his merits to disclose,
Or draw his frailties from their dread abode,
(There they alike in trembling hope repose)
The bosom of his Father and his God.

Oliver Goldsmith from
The Deserted Village

Sweet was the sound when oft at evening's close,
Up yonder hill the village murmur rose;
There as I past with careless steps and slow,
The mingling notes came softened from below;
The swain responsive as the milk-maid sung,
The sober herd that lowed to meet their young;
The noisy geese that gabbled o'er the pool,
The playful children just let loose from school;
The watch-dog's voice that bayed the whispering
     wind,
And the loud laugh that spoke the vacant mind,
These all in sweet confusion sought the shade,
And filled each pause the nightingale had made.
But now the sounds of population fail,
No chearful murmurs fluctuate in the gale,
No busy steps the grass-grown foot-way tread,
For all the bloomy flush of life is fled.
All but yon widowed, solitary thing
That feebly bends beside the plashy spring;
She, wretched matron, forced, in age, for bread,
To strip the brook with mantling cresses spread,
To pick her wintry faggot from the thorn,
To seek her nightly shed, and weep till morn;
She only left of all the harmless train,
The sad historian of the pensive plain.

Near yonder copse, where once the garden smil'd,
And still where many a garden flower grows wild;
There, where a few torn shrubs the place disclose,
The village preacher's modest mansion rose.
A man he was, to all the country dear,
And passing rich with forty pounds a year;
Remote from towns he ran his godly race,
Nor ere had changed, nor wish'd to change his place;
Unpractised he to fawn, or seek for power,
By doctrines fashioned to the varying hour;
Far other aims his heart had learned to prize,
More skilled to raise the wretched than to rise.
His house was known to all the vagrant train,
He chid their wanderings, but relieved their pain;
The long remembered beggar was his guest,
Whose beard descending swept his aged breast;
The ruined spendthrift, now no longer proud,
Claimed kindred there, and had his claims allowed;
The broken soldier, kindly bade to stay,
Sate by his fire, and talked the night away;
Wept o'er his wounds, or tales of sorrow done,
Shouldered his crutch, and shewed how fields were
        won.
Pleased with his guests, the good man learned to
        glow,
And quite forgot their vices in their woe;
Careless their merits, or their faults to scan,
His pity gave ere charity began.

    Thus to relieve the wretched was his pride,
And even his failings leaned to Virtue's side;

But in his duty prompt at every call,
He watched and wept, he prayed and felt, for all.
And, as a bird each fond endearment tries,
To tempt its new fledged offspring to the skies;
He tried each art, reproved each dull delay,
Allured to brighter worlds, and led the way.

Beside the bed where parting life was layed,
And sorrow, guilt, and pain, by turns dismayed,
The reverend champion stood. At his control,
Despair and anguish fled the struggling soul;
Comfort came down the trembling wretch to raise,
And his last faultering accents whispered praise.

At church, with meek and unaffected grace,
His looks adorned the venerable place;
Truth from his lips prevailed with double sway,
And fools, who came to scoff, remained to pray.
The service past, around the pious man,
With steady zeal each honest rustic ran;
Even children followed with endearing wile,
And plucked his gown, to share the good man's
          smile.
His ready smile a parent's warmth exprest,
Their welfare pleased him, and their cares distrest;
To them his heart, his love, his griefs were given,
But all his serious thoughts had rest in Heaven.
As some tall cliff that lifts its awful form
Swells from the vale, and midway leaves the storm,
Tho' round its breast the rolling clouds are spread,
Eternal sunshine settles on its head.

Beside yon straggling fence that skirts the
     way,
With blossomed furze unprofitably gay,
There, in his noisy mansion, skill'd to rule,
The village master taught his little school;
A man severe he was, and stern to view,
I knew him well, and every truant knew;
Well had the boding tremblers learned to trace
The day's disasters in his morning face;
Full well they laugh'd with counterfeited glee,
At all his jokes, for many a joke had he;
Full well the busy whisper circling round,
Conveyed the dismal tidings when he frowned;
Yet he was kind, or if severe in aught,
The love he bore to learning was in fault;
The village all declared how much he knew;
'Twas certain he could write, and cypher too;
Lands he could measure, terms and tides presage,
And even the story ran that he could gauge.
In arguing too, the parson owned his skill,
For even tho' vanquished, he could argue still;
While words of learned length, and thundering
     sound,
Amazed the gazing rustics ranged around,
And still they gazed, and still the wonder grew,
That one small head could carry all he knew.

But past is all his fame. The very spot
Where many a time he triumphed, is forgot.
Near yonder thorn, that lifts its head on high,
Where once the sign-post caught the passing eye,

Low lies that house where nut-brown draughts
        inspired,
Where grey-beard mirth and smiling toil retired,
Where village statesmen talked with looks
        profound,
And news much older than their ale went round.
Imagination fondly stoops to trace
The parlour splendours of that festive place;
The white-washed wall, the nicely sanded floor,
The varnished clock that clicked behind the door;
The chest contrived a double debt to pay,
A bed by night, a chest of drawers by day;
The pictures placed for ornament and use,
The twelve good rules, the royal game of goose;
The hearth, except when winter chill'd the day,
With aspen boughs, and flowers, and fennel gay,
While broken tea-cups, wisely kept for shew,
Ranged o'er the chimney, glistened in a row.

    Vain transitory splendours! Could not all
Reprieve the tottering mansion from its fall!
Obscure it sinks, nor shall it more impart
An hour's importance to the poor man's heart;
Thither no more the peasant shall repair
To sweet oblivion of his daily care;
No more the farmer's news, the barber's tale,
No more the wood-man's ballad shall prevail;
No more the smith his dusky brow shall clear,
Relax his ponderous strength, and lean to hear;
The host himself no longer shall be found
Careful to see the mantling bliss go round;

Nor the coy maid, half willing to be prest,
Shall kiss the cup to pass it to the rest.

Yes! let the rich deride, the proud disdain,
These simple blessings of the lowly train,
To me more dear, congenial to my heart,
One native charm, than all the gloss of art.

William Cowper *The Poplar-Field*

The poplars are fell'd, farewell to the shade
And the whispering sound of the cool colonnade,
The winds play no longer, and sing in the leaves,
Nor Ouse on his bosom their image receives.

Twelve years have elaps'd since I last took a view
Of my favourite field and the bank where they grew,
And now in the grass behold they are laid,
And the tree is my seat that once lent me a shade.

The blackbird has fled to another retreat
Where the hazels afford him a screen from the heat,
And the scene where his melody charm'd me
        before,
Resounds with his sweet-flowing ditty no more.

My fugitive years are all hasting away,
And I must ere long lie as lowly as they,
With a turf on my breast, and a stone at my head,
Ere another such grove shall arise in its stead.

Tis a sight to engage me, if any thing can,
To muse on the perishing pleasures of man;
Though his life be a dream, his enjoyments, I see,
Have a being less durable even than he.

Yardley Oak

Survivor sole, and hardly such, of all
That once liv'd here thy brethren, at my birth
(Since which I number three-score winters past)
A shatter'd veteran, hollow-trunk'd perhaps
As now, and with excoriate forks deform,
Relicts of ages! Could a mind, imbued
With truth from heav'n, created thing adore,
I might with rev'rence kneel and worship thee.

    It seems idolatry with some excuse
When our fore-father Druids in their oaks
Imagin'd sanctity. The conscience yet
Unpurified by an authentic act
Of amnesty, the meed of blood divine,
Lov'd not the light, but gloomy into gloom
Of thickest shades, like Adam after taste
Of fruit proscrib'd, as to a refuge, fled.

    Thou wast a bauble once: a cup and ball,
Which babes might play with; and the thievish jay
Seeking her food, with ease might have purloin'd
The auburn nut that held thee, swallowing down
Thy yet close-folded latitude of boughs
And all thine embryo vastness, at a gulp.
But Fate thy growth decreed: autumnal rains
Beneath thy parent tree mellow'd the soil
Design'd thy cradle, and a skipping deer,

With pointed hoof dibbling the glebe, prepar'd
The soft receptacle in which secure
Thy rudiments should sleep the winter through.

So Fancy dreams – Disprove it, if ye can,
Ye reas'ners broad awake, whose busy searce
Of argument, employ'd too oft amiss,
Sifts half the pleasures of short life away.

Thou fell'st mature, and in the loamy clod
Swelling, with vegetative force instinct
Didst burst thine egg, as theirs the fabled Twins
Now stars; two lobes, protruding, pair'd exact;
A leaf succeeded, and another leaf,
And all the elements thy puny growth
Fost'ring propitious, thou becam'st a twig.

Who liv'd when thou wast such? Oh couldst
    thou speak,
As in Dodona once thy kindred trees
Oracular, I would not curious ask
The future, best unknown, but at thy mouth
Inquisitive, the less ambiguous past.

By thee I might correct, erroneous oft,
The clock of history, facts and events
Timing more punctual, unrecorded facts
Recov'ring, and misstated setting right –
Desp 'rate attempt, till trees shall speak again!

Time made thee what thou wast – King of the
    woods;
And Time hath made thee what thou art – a cave
For owls to roost in. Once thy spreading boughs
O'erhung the champain; and the numerous flock
That graz'd it stood beneath that ample cope

Uncrowded, yet safe-sheltered from the storm.
No flock frequents thee now. Thou hast outliv'd
Thy popularity and art become
(Unless verse rescue thee awhile) a thing
Forgotten, as the foliage of thy youth.
    While thus through all the stages thou hast
        push'd
Of treeship, first a seedling hid in grass,
Then twig, then sapling, and, as century roll'd
Slow after century, a giant bulk
Of girth enormous, with moss-cushion'd root
Upheav'd above the soil, and sides imboss'd
With prominent wens globose, till at the last
The rottenness, which time is charg'd t' inflict
On other mighty ones, found also thee –
What exhibitions various hath the world
Witness'd of mutability in all
That we account most durable below!
Change is the diet, on which all subsist
Created changeable, and change at last
Destroys them. – Skies uncertain now the heat
Transmitting cloudless, and the solar beam
Now quenching in a boundless sea of clouds, –
Calm and alternate storm, moisture and drought,
Invigorate by turns the springs of life
In all that live, plant, animal, and man,
And in conclusion mar them. Nature's threads,
Fine passing thought, ev'n in her coarsest works,
Delight in agitation, yet sustain
The force, that agitates not unimpair'd,
But, worn by frequent impulse, to the cause

Of their best tone their dissolution owe.

    Thought cannot spend itself, comparing still
The great and little of thy lot, thy growth
From almost nullity into a state
Of matchless grandeur, and declension thence
Slow into such magnificent decay.
Time was, when, settling on thy leaf, a fly
Could shake thee to the root – and time has been
When tempests could not. At thy firmest age
Thou hadst within thy bole solid contents
That might have ribb'd the sides or plank'd the
        deck
Of some flagg'd admiral and tortuous arms,
The ship-wright's darling treasure, didst present
To the four-quarter'd winds, robust and bold,
Warp'd into tough knee-timber, many a load.
But the axe spar'd thee; in those thriftier days
Oaks fell not, hewn by thousands, to supply
The bottomless demands of contests wag'd
For senatorial honours. Thus to Time
The task was left to whittle thee away
With his sly scythe, whose ever-nibbling edge
Noiseless, an atom and an atom more
Disjoining from the rest, has, unobserv'd,
Achiev'd a labour, which had, far and wide,
(By man perform'd) made all the forest ring.

    Embowell'd now, and of thy ancient self
Possessing nought but the scoop'd rind, that seems
An huge throat calling to the clouds for drink,
Which it would give in riv'lets to thy root,
Thou temptest none, but rather much forbid'st

The feller's toil, which thou couldst ill requite.
Yet is thy root sincere, sound as the rock,
A quarry of stout spurs and knotted fangs,
Which, crook'd into a thousand whimsies, clasp
The stubborn soil, and hold thee still erect.

So stands a kingdom, whose foundations yet
Fail not, in virtue and in wisdom laid,
Though all the superstructure, by the tooth
Pulveriz'd of venality, a shell
Stands now, and semblance only of itself.

Thine arms have left thee. Winds have rent
          them off
Long since, and rovers of the forest wild
With bow and shaft have burnt them. Some have
          left
A splinter'd stump bleach'd to a snowy white;
And some memorial none where once they grew.
Yet life still lingers in thee, and puts forth
Proof not contemptible of what she can,
Even where death predominates. The spring
Thee finds not less alive to her sweet force
Than yonder upstarts of the neighbour wood,
So much thy juniors, who their birth receiv'd
Half a millennium since the date of thine.

But since, although well qualified by age
To teach, no spirit dwells in thee, nor voice
May be expected from thee, seated here
On thy distorted root, with hearers none
Or prompter, save the scene, I will perform
Myself the oracle and will discourse
In my own ear such matter as I may.

Thou, like myself, hast stage by stage attain'd
Life's wintry bourn; thou, after many years,
I after few; but few or many prove
A span in retrospect; for I can touch
With my least finger's end my own decease
And with extended thumb my natal hour,
And hadst thou also skill in measurement
As I, the past would seem as short to thee.
Evil and few – said Jacob – at an age
Thrice mine, and few and evil, I may think
The Prediluvian race, whose buxom youth
Endured two centuries, accounted theirs.
'Shortliv'd as foliage is the race of man.
The wind shakes down the leaves, the budding
      grove
Soon teems with others, and in spring they grow.
So pass mankind. One generation meets
Its destin'd period, and a new succeeds.'
Such was the tender but undue complaint
Of the Mæonian in old time; for who
Would drawl out centuries in tedious strife
Severe with mental and corporeal ill
And would not rather chuse a shorter race
To glory, a few decads here below?

   One man alone, the Father of us all,
Drew not his life from woman; never gaz'd,
With mute unconsciousness of what he saw
On all around him; learn'd not by degrees,
Nor owed articulation to his ear;
But, moulded by his Maker into Man
At once, upstood intelligent, survey'd

All creatures, with precision understood
Their purport, uses, properties, assign'd
To each his name significant, and, fill'd
With love and wisdom, render'd back to heav'n
In praise harmonious the first air he drew.
He was excus'd the penalties of dull
Minority. No tutor charg'd his hand
With the thought-tracing quill, or task'd his mind
With problems; history, not wanted yet,
Lean'd on her elbow, watching Time, whose
        course,
Eventful, should supply her with a theme;

[unfinished]

from The Task, Book Five

'Tis morning; and the sun, with ruddy orb
Ascending, fires th' horizon: while the clouds,
That crowd away before the driving wind,
More ardent as the disk emerges more,
Resemble most some city in a blaze,
Seen through the leafless wood. His slanting ray
Slides ineffectual down the snowy vale,
And, tinging all with his own rosy hue,
From ev'ry herb and ev'ry spiry blade
Stretches a length of shadow o'er the field.
Mine, spindling into longitude immense,
In spite of gravity, and sage remark
That I myself am but a fleeting shade,
Provokes me to a smile. With eye askance
I view the muscular proportion'd limb
Transform'd to a lean shank. The shapeless pair,
As they design'd to mock me, at my side
Take step for step; and, as I near approach
The cottage, walk along the plaster'd wall,
Prepost'rous sight! the legs without the man.
The verdure of the plain lies buried deep
Beneath the dazzling deluge; and the bents,
And coarser grass, upspearing o'er the rest,
Of late unsightly and unseen, now shine
Conspicuous, and, in bright apparel clad

And fledg'd with icy feathers, nod superb.
The cattle mourn in corners where the fence
Screens them, and seem half petrified to sleep
In unrecumbent sadness. There they wait
Their wonted fodder, not like hung'ring man,
Fretful if unsupply'd; but silent, meek,
And patient of the slow-pac'd swain's delay.
He from the stack carves out th' accustom'd load,
Deep-plunging, and again deep-plunging oft,
His broad keen knife into the solid mass:
Smooth as a wall the upright remnant stands,
With such undeviating and even force
He severs it away: no needless care,
Lest storms should overset the leaning pile
Deciduous, or its own unbalanc'd weight.
Forth goes the woodman, leaving unconcern'd
The cheerful haunts of man; to wield the axe
And drive the wedge, in yonder forest drear,
From morn to eve his solitary task.
Shaggy, and lean, and shrewd, with pointed ears
And tail cropp'd short, half lurcher and half cur –
His dog attends him. Close behind his heel
Now creeps he slow; and now, with many a frisk
Wide-scamp'ring, snatches up the drifted snow
With iv'ry teeth, or ploughs it with his snout;
Then shakes his powder'd coat, and barks for joy.
Heedless of all his pranks, the sturdy churl
Moves right toward the mark; nor stops for aught,
But now and then with pressure of a thumb
T' adjust the fragrant charge of a short tube
That fumes beneath the nose; the trailing cloud

44

Streams far behind him, scenting all the air.
Now from the roost, or from the neighb'ring pale,
Where, diligent to catch the first faint gleam
Of smiling day, they gossip'd side by side,
Come trooping at the housewife's well-known call
The feather'd tribes domestic. Half on wing,
And half on foot, they brush the fleecy flood,
Conscious, and fearful of too deep a plunge.
The sparrows peep, and quit the shelt'ring eaves
To seize the fair occasion. Well they eye
The scatter'd grain; and, thievishly resolv'd
T' escape th' impending famine, often scar'd,
As oft return – a pert voracious kind.
Clean riddance quickly made, one only care
Remains to each – the search of sunny nook,
Or shed impervious to the blast. Resign'd
To sad necessity, the cock foregoes
His wonted strut and, wading at their head
With well-consider'd steps, seems to resent
His alter'd gait and stateliness retrench'd.
How find the myriads, that in summer cheer
The hills and vallies with their ceaseless songs,
Due sustenance, or where subsist they now?
Earth yields them nought: th' imprison'd worm is
      safe
Beneath the frozen clod; all seeds of herbs
Lie cover'd close; and berry-bearing thorns,
That feed the thrush, (whatever some suppose)
Afford the smaller minstrels no supply.
The long protracted rigour of the year
Thins all their num 'rous flocks. In chinks and holes

Ten thousand seek an unmolested end,
As instinct prompts; self-buried ere they die.
The very rooks and daws forsake the fields,
Where neither grub, nor root, nor earth-nut, now
Repays their labour more; and, perch'd aloft
By the way-side, or stalking in the path,
Lean pensioners upon the trav'ler's track,
Pick up their nauseous dole, though sweet to them,
Of voided pulse or half-digested grain.
The streams are lost amid the splendid blank,
O'erwhelming all distinction. On the flood,
Indurated and fixt, the snowy weight
Lies undissolv'd; while silently beneath,
And unperceiv'd, the current steals away.
Not so where, scornful of a check, it leaps
The mill-dam, dashes on the restless wheel,
And wantons in the pebbly gulph below:
No frost can bind it there; its utmost force
Can but arrest the light and smoky mist
That in its fall the liquid sheet throws wide.
And see where it has hung th' embroider'd banks
With forms so various, that no pow'rs of art,
The pencil or the pen, may trace the scene!
Here glitt'ring turrets rise, upbearing high
(Fantastic misarrangement!) on the roof
Large growth of what may seem the sparkling trees
And shrubs of fairy land. The crystal drops
That trickle down the branches, fast congeal'd,
Shoot into pillars of pellucid length,
And prop the pile they but adorn'd before.
Here grotto within grotto safe defies

The sun-beam; there, emboss'd and fretted wild,
The growing wonder takes a thousand shapes
Capricious, in which fancy seeks in vain
The likeness of some object seen before.
Thus nature works as if to mock at art,
And in defiance of her rival pow'rs;
By these fortuitous and random strokes
Performing such inimitable feats
As she with all her rules can never reach.
Less worthy of applause, though more admir'd,
Because of novelty, the work of man,
Imperial mistress of the fur-clad Russ!
Thy most magnificent and mighty freak,
The wonder of the North. No forest fell
When thou wouldst build; no quarry sent its stores
T' enrich thy walls: but thou didst hew the floods,
And make thy marble of the glassy wave.
In such a palace Aristæus found
Cyrene, when he bore the plaintive tale
Of his lost bees to her maternal ear:
In such a palace poetry might place
The armory of winter; where his troops
The gloomy clouds, find weapons, arrowy sleet,
Skin-piercing volley, blossom-bruising hail,
And snow that often blinds the trav'ler's course,
And wraps him in an unexpected tomb.
Silently as a dream the fabric rose; –
No sound of hammer or of saw was there:
Ice upon ice, the well-adjusted parts
Were soon conjoin'd; nor other cement ask'd
Than water interfus'd to make them one.

Lamps gracefully dispos'd, and of all hues,
Illumin'd ev'ry side: a wat'ry light
Gleam'd through the clear transparency, that
    seem'd
Another moon new risen, or meteor fall'n
From heav'n to earth, of lambent flame serene.
So stood the brittle prodigy; though smooth
And slipp'ry the materials, yet frost-bound
Firm as a rock. Nor wanted aught within,
That royal residence might well befit,
For grandeur or for use. Long wavy wreaths
Of flow'rs, that fear'd no enemy but warmth,
Blush'd on the pannels. Mirror needed none
Where all was vitreous; but in order due
Convivial table and commodious seat
(What seem'd at least commodious seat) were
    there;
Sofa, and couch, and high-built throne august.
The same lubricity was found in all,
And all was moist to the warm touch; a scene
Of evanescent glory, once a stream,
And soon to glide into a stream again.
Alas! 'twas but a mortifying stroke
Of undesign'd severity, that glanc'd
(Made by a monarch) on her own estate,
On human grandeur and the courts of kings.
'Twas transient in its nature, as in show
'Twas durable: as worthless, as it seem'd
Intrinsically precious to the foot
Treach'rous and false; it smil'd, and it was cold.

William Wordsworth A Night-Piece

               The sky is overspread
With a close veil of one continuous cloud
All whitened by the moon, that just appears,
A dim-seen orb, yet chequers not the ground
With any shadow – plant, or tower, or tree.
At last a pleasant instantaneous light
Startles the musing man whose eyes are bent
To earth. He looks around, the clouds are split
Asunder, and above his head he views
The clear moon and the glory of the heavens.
There in a black-blue vault she sails along
Followed by multitudes of stars, that small,
And bright, and sharp along the gloomy vault
Drive as she drives. How fast they wheel away!
Yet vanish not! The wind is in the trees;
But they are silent. Still they roll along
Immeasurably distant, and the vault
Built round by those white clouds, enormous
     clouds,
Still deepens its interminable depth.
At length the vision closes, and the mind
Not undisturbed by the deep joy it feels,
Which slowly settles into peaceful calm,
Is left to muse upon the solemn seene.

Lines Written A Few Miles Above Tintern Abbey On Revisiting the Banks of the Wye During a Tour, July 13, 1798

Five years have passed; five summers, with the length
Of five long winters! and again I hear
These waters, rolling from their mountain-springs
With a sweet inland murmur. – Once again
Do I behold these steep and lofty cliffs,
Which on a wild secluded scene impress
Thoughts of more deep seclusion; and connect
The landscape with the quiet of the sky.
The day is come when I again repose
Here, under this dark sycamore, and view
These plots of cottage-ground, these orchard-tufts,
Which, at this season, with their unripe fruits,
Among the woods and copses lose themselves,
Nor, with their green and simple hue, disturb
The wild green landscape. Once again I see
These hedge-rows, hardly hedge-rows, little lines
Of sportive wood run wild; these pastoral farms
Green to the very door; and wreathes of smoke
Sent up, in silence, from among the trees,
With some uncertain notice, as might seem,
Of vagrant dwellers in the houseless woods,
Or of some hermit's cave, where by his fire
The hermit sits alone.

                              Though absent long,
These forms of beauty have not been to me,
As is a landscape to a blind man's eye:
But oft, in lonely rooms, and mid the din
Of towns and cities, I have owed to them,
In hours of weariness, sensations sweet,
Felt in the blood, and felt along the heart,
And passing even into my purer mind
With tranquil restoration: – feelings too
Of unremembered pleasure; such, perhaps,
As may have had no trivial influence
On that best portion of a good man's life;
His little, nameless, unremembered acts
Of kindness and of love. Nor less, I trust,
To them I may have owed another gift,
Of aspect more sublime; that blessed mood,
In which the burthen of the mystery,
In which the heavy and the weary weight
Of all this unintelligible world
Is lightened: – that serene and blessed mood,
In which the affections gently lead us on,
Until, the breath of this corporeal frame,
And even the motion of our human blood
Almost suspended, we are laid asleep
In body, and become a living soul:
While with an eye made quiet by the power
Of harmony, and the deep power of joy,
We see into the life of things.

                              If this
Be but a vain belief, yet, oh! how oft,

In darkness, and amid the many shapes
Of joyless day-light; when the fretful stir
Unprofitable, and the fever of the world,
Have hung upon the beatings of my heart,
How oft, in spirit, have I turned to thee
O sylvan Wye! Thou wanderer through the woods,
How often has my spirit turned to thee!

And now, with gleams of half-extinguished thought,
With many recognitions dim and faint,
And somewhat of a sad perplexity,
The picture of the mind revives again:
While here I stand, not only with the sense
Of present pleasure, but with pleasing thoughts
That in this moment there is life and food
For future years. And so I dare to hope
Though changed, no doubt, from what I was, when first
I came among these hills; when like a roe
I bounded o'er the mountains, by the sides
Of the deep rivers, and the lonely streams,
Wherever nature led; more like a man
Flying from something that he dreads, than one
Who sought the thing he loved. For nature then
(The coarser pleasures of my boyish days,
And their glad animal movements all gone by,)
To me was all in all. — I cannot paint
What then I was. The sounding cataract
Haunted me like a passion: the tall rock,
The mountain, and the deep and gloomy wood,
Their colours and their forms, were then to me
An appetite: a feeling and a love,

That had no need of a remoter charm,
By thought supplied, or any interest
Unborrowed from the eye. – That time is past,
And all its aching joys are now no more,
And all its dizzy raptures. Not for this
Faint I, nor mourn nor murmur: other gifts
Have followed, for such loss, I would believe,
Abundant recompence. For I have learned
To look on nature, not as in the hour
Of thoughtless youth, but hearing oftentimes
The still, sad music of humanity,
Not harsh nor grating, though of ample power
To chasten and subdue. And I have felt
A presence that disturbs me with the joy
Of elevated thoughts; a sense sublime
Of something far more deeply interfused,
Whose dwelling is the light of setting suns,
And the round ocean, and the living air,
And the blue sky, and in the mind of man,
A motion and a spirit, that impels
All thinking things, all objects of all thought,
And rolls through all things. Therefore am I still
A lover of the meadows and the woods,
And mountains; and of all that we behold
From this green earth; of all the mighty world
Of eye and ear, both what they half-create,
And what perceive; well pleased to recognize
In nature and the language of the sense,
The anchor of my purest thoughts, the nurse,
The guide, the guardian of my heart, and soul
Of all my moral being.

                    Nor, perchance,
If I were not thus taught, should I the more
Suffer my genial spirits to decay:
For thou art with me, here, upon the banks
Of this fair river; thou, my dearest Friend,
My dear, dear Friend, and in thy voice I catch
The language of my former heart, and read
My former pleasures in the shooting lights
Of thy wild eyes. Oh! yet a little while
May I behold in thee what I was once,
My dear, dear Sister! And this prayer I make,
Knowing that Nature never did betray
The heart that loved her; 'tis her privilege,
Through all the years of this our life, to lead
From joy to joy: for she can so inform
The mind that is within us, so impress
With quietness and beauty, and so feed
With lofty thoughts, that neither evil tongues,
Rash judgments, nor the sneers of selfish men,
Nor greetings where no kindness is, nor all
The dreary intercourse of daily life,
Shall e'er prevail against us, or disturb
Our chearful faith that all which we behold
Is full of blessings. Therefore let the moon
Shine on thee in thy solitary walk;
And let the misty mountain winds be free
To blow against thee: and in after years,
When these wild ecstasies shall be matured
Into a sober pleasure, when thy mind
Shall be a mansion for all lovely forms,
Thy memory be as a dwelling-place

For all sweet sounds and harmonies; Oh! then,
If solitude, or fear, or pain, or grief,
Should be thy portion, with what healing thoughts
Of tender joy wilt thou remember me,
And these my exhortations! Nor, perchance,
If I should be, where I no more can hear
Thy voice, nor catch from thy wild eyes these
    gleams
Of past existence, wilt thou then forget
That on the banks of this delightful stream
We stood together; and that I, so long
A worshipper of Nature, hither came,
Unwearied in that service: rather say
With warmer love, oh! with far deeper zeal
Of holier love. Nor wilt thou then forget,
That after many wanderings, many years
Of absence, these steep woods and lofty cliffs,
And this green pastoral landscape, were to me
More dear, both for themselves, and for thy
    sake.

'I wandered lonely as a Cloud'

I wandered lonely as a Cloud
That floats on high o'er Vales and Hills,
When all at once I saw a crowd
A host of dancing Daffodils;
Along the Lake, beneath the trees,
Ten thousand dancing in the breeze.

The waves beside them danced, but they
Outdid the sparkling waves in glee: –
A Poet could not but be gay
In such a laughing company:
I gazed – and gazed – but little thought
What wealth the shew to me had brought:

For oft when on my couch I lie
In vacant or in pensive mood,
They flash upon that inward eye
Which is the bliss of solitude,
And then my heart with pleasure fills,
And dances with the Daffodils.

Yew-Trees

There is a Yew-tree, pride of Lorton Vale,
Which to this day stands single, in the midst
Of its own darkness, as it stood of yore,
Not loth to furnish weapons for the Bands
Of Umfraville or Percy ere they marched
To Scotland's Heaths; or Those that crossed the
    Sea
And drew their sounding bows at Azincour,
Perhaps at earlier Crecy, or Poictiers.
Of vast circumference and gloom profound
This solitary Tree! – a living thing
Produced too slowly ever to decay;
Of form and aspect too magnificent
To be destroyed. But worthier still of note
Are those fraternal Four of Borrowdale,
Joined in one solemn and capacious grove;
Huge trunks! – and each particular trunk a growth
Of intertwisted fibres serpentine
Up-coiling, and inveterately convolved, –
Nor uninformed with Phantasy, and looks
That threaten the prophane; – a pillared shade,
Upon whose grassless floor of red-brown hue,
By sheddings from the pining umbrage tinged
Perennially – beneath whose sable roof
Of boughs, as if for festal purpose, decked

With unrejoicing berries, ghostly Shapes
May meet at noontide – Fear and trembling Hope,
Silence and Foresight – Death the Skeleton
And Time the Shadow, – there to celebrate,
As in a natural temple scattered o'er
With altars undisturbed of mossy stone,
United worship; or in mute repose
To lie, and listen to the mountain flood
Murmuring from Glaramara's inmost caves.

from The Prelude, Book Eleven
Imagination, How Impaired and Restored

There are in our existence spots of time,
Which with distinct pre-eminence retain
A renovating Virtue, whence, depressed
By false opinion and contentious thought,
Or aught of heavier and more deadly weight
In trivial occupations, and the round
Of ordinary intercourse, our minds
Are nourished and invisibly repaired;
A virtue by which pleasure is enhanced,
That penetrates, enables us to mount
When high, more high, and lifts us up when fallen.
This efficacious spirit chiefly lurks
Among those passages of life in which
We have had deepest feeling that the mind
Is lord and master, and that outward sense
Is but the obedient servant of her will.
Such moments worthy of all gratitude,
Are scattered everywhere, taking their date
From our first childhood: in our childhood even
Perhaps are most conspicuous. Life with me,
As far as memory can look back, is full
Of this beneficent influence.
                                        At a time
When scarcely (I was then not six years old)
My hand could hold a bridle, with proud hopes

I mounted, and we rode towards the hills:
We were a pair of Horsemen; honest James
Was with me, my encourager and guide.
We had not travelled long ere some mischance
Disjoined me from my Comrade, and, through fear
Dismounting, down the rough and stony Moor
I led my Horse, and stumbling on, at length
Came to a bottom, where in former times
A Murderer had been hung in iron chains.
The Gibbet-mast was mouldered down, the bones
And iron case were gone, but on the turf,
Hard by, soon after that fell deed was wrought,
Some unknown hand had carved the Murderer's
    name.
The monumental writing was engraven
In times long past, and still from year to year
By superstition of the neighbourhood
The grass is cleared away; and to this hour
The letters are all fresh and visible.
Faltering, and ignorant where I was, at length
I chanced to espy those characters inscribed
On the green sod: forthwith I left the spot
And, reascending the bare Common, saw
A naked Pool that lay beneath the hills,
The Beacon on the summit, and more near,
A Girl who bore a Pitcher on her head
And seemed with difficult steps to force her way
Against the blowing wind. It was, in truth,
An ordinary sight; but I should need
Colours and words that are unknown to man
To paint the visionary dreariness

Which, while I looked all round for my lost guide,
Did at that time invest the naked Pool,
The Beacon on the lonely Eminence,
The Woman, and her garments vexed and tossed
By the strong wind. When, in a blessed season
With those two dear Ones, to my heart so dear,
When in the blessed time of early love,
Long afterwards, I roamed about
In daily presence of this very scene,
Upon the naked pool and dreary crags,
And on the melancholy Beacon, fell
The spirit of pleasure and youth's golden gleam;
And think ye not with radiance more divine
From these remembrances, and from the power
They left behind? So feeling comes in aid
Of feeling, and diversity of strength
Attends us, if but once we have been strong.
Oh! mystery of Man, from what a depth
Proceed thy honours! I am lost, but see
In simple childhood something of the base
On which thy greatness stands; but this I feel,
That from thyself it is that thou must give,
Else never canst receive. The days gone by
Come back upon me from the dawn almost
Of life: the hiding-places of my power
Seem open; I approach, and then they close;
I see by glimpses now; when age comes on,
May scarcely see at all, and I would give,
While yet we may, as far as words can give,
A substance and a life to what I feel:
I would enshrine the spirit of the past

For future restoration. Yet another
Of these to me affecting incidents
With which we will conclude.

                              One Christmas-time,
The day before the Holidays began,
Feverish, and tired, and restless, I went forth
Into the fields, impatient for the sight
Of those two Horses which should bear us home,
My Brothers and myself. There was a crag,
An Eminence, which from the meeting-point
Of two highways ascending, overlooked
At least a long half-mile of those two roads,
By each of which the expected Steeds might come,
The choice uncertain. Thither I repaired
Up to the highest summit. 'Twas a day
Stormy, and rough, and wild, and on the grass
I sate, half-sheltered by a naked wall;
Upon my right hand was a single sheep,
A whistling hawthorn on my left, and there,
With those companions at my side, I watched,
Straining my eyes intensely, as the mist
Gave intermitting prospect of the wood
And plain beneath. Ere I to School returned
That dreary time, ere I had been ten days
A dweller in my Father's House, he died,
And I and my two Brothers, Orphans then,
Followed his Body to the Grave. The event
With all the sorrow which it brought appeared
A chastisement; and when I called to mind
That day so lately passed, when from the crag
I looked in such anxiety of hope,

With trite reflections of morality,
Yet in the deepest passion, I bowed low
To God, who thus corrected my desires;
And afterwards, the wind and sleety rain,
And all the business of the elements,
The single sheep, and the one blasted tree,
And the bleak music of that old stone wall,
The noise of wood and water, and the mist
Which on the line of each of those two Roads
Advanced in such indisputable shapes,
All these were spectacles and sounds to which
I often would repair and thence would drink
As at a fountain; and I do not doubt
That in this later time, when storm and rain
Beat on my roof at midnight, or by day
When I am in the woods, unknown to me
The workings of my spirit thence are brought.

Samuel Taylor Coleridge
This Lime-Tree Bower My Prison

In the June of 1797 some long-expected friends paid a visit to the author's cottage; and on the morning of their arrival, he met with an accident, which disabled him from walking during the whole time of their stay. One evening, when they had left him for a few hours, he composed the following lines in the garden-bower.

Well, they are gone, and here must I remain,
This lime-tree bower my prison! I have lost
Beauties and feelings, such as would have been
Most sweet to my remembrance even when age
Had dimm'd mine eyes to blindness! They,
    meanwhile,
Friends, whom I never more may meet again,
On springy heath, along the hill-top edge,
Wander in gladness, and wind down, perchance,
To that still roaring dell, of which I told;
The roaring dell, o'erwooded, narrow, deep,
And only speckled by the mid-day sun;
Where its slim trunk the ash from rock to rock
Flings arching like a bridge; – that branchless ash,
Unsunn'd and damp, whose few poor yellow leaves
Ne'er tremble in the gale, yet tremble still,
Fann'd by the water-fall! and there my friends

Behold the dark green file of long lank weeds,
That all at once (a most fantastic sight!)
Still nod and drip beneath the dripping edge
Of the blue clay-stone.

                    Now, my friends emerge
Beneath the wide wide Heaven – and view again
The many-steepled tract magnificent
Of hilly fields and meadows, and the sea,
With some fair bark, perhaps, whose sails light up
The slip of smooth clear blue betwixt two Isles
Of purple shadow! Yes! they wander on
In gladness all; but thou, methinks, most glad,
My gentle-hearted Charles! for thou hast pined
And hunger'd after Nature, many a year,
In the great City pent, winning thy way
With sad yet patient soul, through evil and pain
And strange calamity! Ah! slowly sink
Behind the western ridge, thou glorious Sun!
Shine in the slant beams of the sinking orb,
Ye purple heath-flowers! richlier burn, ye clouds!
Live in the yellow light, ye distant groves!
And kindle, thou blue Ocean! So my friend
Struck with deep joy may stand, as I have stood,
Silent with swimming sense; yea, gazing round
On the wide landscape, gaze till all doth seem
Less gross than bodily; and of such hues
As veil the Almighty Spirit, when yet he makes
Spirits perceive his presence.

                              A delight
Comes sudden on my heart, and I am glad
As I myself were there! Nor in this bower,
This little lime-tree bower, have I not mark'd
Much that has sooth'd me. Pale beneath the blaze
Hung the transparent foliage; and I watch'd
Some broad and sunny leaf, and lov'd to see
The shadow of the leaf and stem above
Dappling its sunshine! And that walnut-tree
Was richly ting'd, and a deep radiance lay
Full on the ancient ivy, which usurps
Those fronting elms, and now, with blackest mass
Makes their dark branches gleam a lighter hue
Through the late twilight: and though now the bat
Wheels silent by, and not a swallow twitters,
Yet still the solitary humble-bee
Sings in the bean-flower! Henceforth I shall know
That Nature ne'er deserts the wise and pure;
No plot so narrow, be but Nature there,
No waste so vacant, but may well employ
Each faculty of sense, and keep the heart
Awake to Love and Beauty! and sometimes
'Tis well to be bereft of promis'd good,
That we may lift the soul, and contemplate
With lively joy the joys we cannot share.
My gentle-hearted Charles! when the last rook
Beat its straight path along the dusky air
Homewards, I blest it! deeming its black wing
(Now a dim speck, now vanishing in light)
Had cross'd the mighty Orb's dilated glory,
While thou stood'st gazing; or, when all was still,

Flew creeking o'er thy head, and had a charm
For thee, my gentle-hearted Charles, to whom
No sound is dissonant which tells of Life.

Lines Composed while Climbing the Left Ascent of Brockley Coomb, Somersetshire, May 1795

With many a pause and oft reverted eye
I climb the Coomb's ascent: sweet songsters near
Warble in shade their wild-wood melody:
Far off the unvarying Cuckoo soothes my ear.
Up scour the startling stragglers of the flock
That on green plots o'er precipices browze:
From the deep fissures of the naked rock
The Yew-tree bursts! Beneath its dark green boughs
(Mid which the May-thorn blends its blossoms white)
Where broad smooth stones jut out in mossy seats,
I rest: – and now have gain'd the topmost site.
Ah! what a luxury of landscape meets
My gaze! Proud towers, and Cots more dear to me,
Elm-shadow'd Fields, and prospect-bounding Sea!
Deep sighs my lonely heart: I drop the tear:
Enchanting spot! O were my Sara here!

John Clare
Emmonsails Heath in Winter

I love to see the old heath's withered brake
Mingle its crimpled leaves with furze and ling
While the old heron from the lonely lake
Starts slow and flaps his melancholy wing
And oddling crow in idle motions swing
On the half-rotten ash tree's topmost twig
Beside whose trunk the gypsy makes his bed –
Up flies the bouncing woodcock from the brig
Where a black quagmire quakes beneath the tread;
The fieldfare chatters in the whistling thorn
And for the 'awe round fields and closen rove,
And coy bumbarrels twenty in a drove
Flit down the hedgerows in the frozen plain
And hang on little twigs and start again.

The Nightingale's Nest

Up this green woodland-ride let's softly rove
And list the nightingale – she dwells just here.
Hush! let the wood-gate softly clap for fear
The noise might drive her from her home of love,
For here I've heard her many a merry year –
At morn, at eve, nay, all the livelong day,
As though she lived on song. This very spot,
Just where that old-man's-beard all wildly trails
Rude arbours o'er the road and stops the way –
And where that child its bluebell flowers hath got,
Laughing and creeping through the mossy rails –
There have I hunted like a very boy,
Creeping on hands and knees through matted thorn
To find her nest and see her feed her young.
And vainly did I many hours employ:
All seemed as hidden as a thought unborn.
And where those crimping fern-leaves ramp among
The hazel's under-boughs, I've nestled down
And watched her while she sung, and her renown
Hath made me marvel that so famed a bird
Should have no better dress than russet brown.
Her wings would tremble in her ecstasy
And feathers stand on end as 'twere with joy
And mouth wide open to release her heart
Of its out-sobbing songs. The happiest part

Of summer's fame she shared, for so to me
Did happy fancies shapen her employ,
But if I touched a bush or scarcely stirred,
All in a moment stopped. I watched in vain:
The timid bird had left the hazel bush
And at a distance hid to sing again.
Lost in a wilderness of listening leaves,
Rich ecstasy would pour its luscious strain
Till envy spurred the emulating thrush
To start less wild and scarce inferior songs,
For while of half the year care him bereaves
To damp the ardour of his speckled breast,
The nightingale to summer's life belongs
And naked trees and winter's nipping wrongs
Are strangers to her music and her rest.
Her joys are evergreen, her world is wide –
Hark! there she is as usual – let's be hush –
For in this blackthorn-clump, if rightly guessed,
Her curious house is hidden. Part aside
These hazel branches in a gentle way
And stoop right cautious 'neath the rustling boughs,
For we will have another search today
And hunt this fern-strewn thorn clump round and
    round,
And where this seeded wood-grass idly bows
We'll wade right through, it is a likely nook:
In such like spots and often on the ground,
They'll build, where rude boys never think to look.
Ay, as I live – her secret nest is here,
Upon this whitethorn stulp. I've searched about
For hours in vain – there, put that bramble by –

Nay, trample on its branches and get near.
How subtle is the bird! she started out
And raised a plaintive note of danger nigh
Ere we were past the brambles, and now, near
Her nest, she sudden stops – as choking fear
That might betray her home. So even now
We'll leave it as we found it: safety's guard
Of pathless solitudes shall keep it still.
See there – she's sitting on the old oak bough,
Mute in her fears; our presence doth retard
Her joys, and doubt turns every rapture chill.
Sing on, sweet bird, may no worse hap befall
Thy visions than the fear that now deceives.
We will not plunder music of its dower
Nor turn this spot of happiness to thrall,
For melody seems hid in every flower
That blossoms near thy home – these harebells all
Seem bowing with the beautiful in song
And gaping cuckoo-flower with spotted leaves
Seems blushing with the singing it has heard.
How curious is the nest: no other bird
Uses such loose materials or weaves
Its dwelling in such spots – dead oaken leaves
Are placed without and velvet moss within
And little scraps of grass and, scant and spare,
What scarcely seem materials, down and hair.
For from man's haunts she nothing seems to win,
Yet nature is the builder and contrives
Homes for her children's comfort even here
Where solitude's disciples spend their lives
Unseen, save when a wanderer passes near

That loves such pleasant places. Deep adown
The nest is made, a hermit's mossy cell.
Snug lie her curious eggs in number five
Of deadened green or rather olive-brown,
And the old prickly thorn-bush guards them well.
So here we'll leave them, still unknown to wrong,
As the old woodland's legacy of song.

'The old pond full of flags and fenced around'

The old pond full of flags and fenced around
With trees and bushes trailing to the ground
The water weeds are all around the brink
And one clear place where cattle go to drink
From year to year the schoolboy thither steals
And muddys round the place to catch the eels
The cowboy often hiding from the flies
Lies there and plaits the rushcap as he lies
The hissing owl sits moping all the day
And hears his song and never flies away
The pinks nest hangs upon the branch so thin
The young ones caw and seem as tumbling in
While round them thrums the purple dragon flye
And great white butter flye goes dancing bye

John Keats To Autumn

Season of mists and mellow fruitfulness,
    Close bosom-friend of the maturing sun;
Conspiring with him how to load and bless
    With fruit the vines that round the thatch-eves
        run;
To bend with apples the moss'd cottage-trees,
    And fill all fruit with ripeness to the core;
        To swell the gourd, and plump the hazel
           shells
With a sweet kernel; to set budding more,
    And still more, later flowers for the bees,
    Until they think warm days will never cease,
        For Summer has o'er-brimm'd their clammy
           cells.

Who hath not seen thee oft amid thy store?
    Sometimes whoever seeks abroad may find
Thee sitting careless on a granary floor,
    Thy hair soft-lifted by the winnowing wind;
Or on a half-reap'd furrow sound asleep,
    Drows'd with the fume of poppies, while thy
        hook
        Spares the next swath and all its twined
           flowers:
And sometimes like a gleaner thou dost keep

Steady thy laden head across a brook;
Or by a cyder-press, with patient look,
   Thou watchest the last oozings hours by
      hours.

Where are the songs of Spring? Ay, where are
      they?
   Think not of them, thou hast thy music too, –
While barred clouds bloom the soft-dying day,
   And touch the stubble-plains with rosy hue;
Then in a wailful choir the small gnats mourn
   Among the river shallows, borne aloft
     Or sinking as the light wind lives or dies;
And full-grown lambs loud bleat from hilly bourn;
   Hedge-crickets sing; and now with treble soft
   The red-breast whistles from a garden-croft;
     And gathering swallows twitter in the skies.

Emily Brontë
'The night is darkening round me'

The night is darkening round me
The wild winds coldly blow
But a tyrant spell has bound me
And I cannot cannot go

The giant trees are bending
Their bare boughs weighed with snow
And the storm is fast descending
And yet I cannot go

Clouds beyond clouds above me
Wastes beyond wastes below
But nothing drear can move me
I will not cannot go

'The blue bell is the sweetest flower'

The blue bell is the sweetest flower
That waves in summer air
Its blossoms have the mightiest power
To soothe my spirit's care

There is a spell in purple heath
Too wildly, sadly drear
The violet has a fragrant breath
But fragrance will not cheer

The trees are bare, the sun is cold
And seldom, seldom seen –
The heavens have lost their zone of gold
The earth its robe of green

And ice upon the glancing stream
Has cast its sombre shade
And distant hills and valleys seem
In frozen mist arrayed –

The blue bell cannot charm me now
The heath has lost its bloom
The violets in the glen below
They yield no sweet perfume

But though I mourn the heather-bell
'Tis better far, away
I know how fast my tears would swell
To see it smile today

And that wood flower that hides so shy
Beneath the mossy stone
Its balmy scent and dewy eye
'Tis not for them I moan

It is the slight and stately stem
The blossom's silvery blue
The buds hid like a sapphire gem
In sheaths of emerald hue

Thomas Hardy *A Sheep Fair*

The day arrives of the autumn fair,
    And torrents fall,
Though sheep in throngs are gathered there,
    Ten thousand all,
Sodden, with hurdles round them reared:
And, lot by lot, the pens are cleared,
And the auctioneer wrings out his beard,
And wipes his book, bedrenched and smeared,
And rakes the rain from his face with the edge of
        his hand,
    As torrents fall.

The wool of the ewes is like a sponge
    With the daylong rain:
Jammed tight, to turn, or lie, or lunge,
    They strive in vain.
Their horns are soft as finger-nails,
Their shepherds reek against the rails,
The tied dogs soak with tucked-in tails,
The buyers' hat-brims fill like pails,
Which spill small cascades when they shift their
        stand
    In the daylong rain.

POSTSCRIPT

Time has trailed lengthily since met
    At Pummery Fair
Those panting thousands in their wet
    And woolly wear:
And every flock long since has bled,
And all the dripping buyers have sped,
And the hoarse auctioneer is dead,
Who 'Going – going!' so often said,
As he consigned to doom each meek, mewed band
    At Pummery Fair.

The Darkling Thrush

I leant upon a coppice gate
    When Frost was spectre-gray,
And Winter's dregs made desolate
    The weakening eye of day.
The tangled bine-stems scored the sky
    Like strings of broken lyres,
And all mankind that haunted nigh
    Had sought their household fires.

The land's sharp features seemed to be
    The Century's corpse outleant,
His crypt the cloudy canopy,
    The wind his death-lament.
The ancient pulse of germ and birth
    Was shrunken hard and dry,
And every spirit upon earth
    Seemed fervourless as I.

At once a voice arose among
    The bleak twigs overhead
In a full-hearted evensong
    Of joy illimited;
An aged thrush, frail, gaunt, and small,
    In blast-beruffled plume,
Had chosen thus to fling his soul
    Upon the growing gloom.

So little cause for carolings
    Of such ecstatic sound
Was written on terrestrial things
    Afar or nigh around,
That I could think there trembled through
    His happy good-night air
Some blessed Hope, whereof he knew
    And I was unaware.

Channel Firing

That night your great guns, unawares,
Shook all our coffins as we lay,
And broke the chancel window-squares,
We thought it was the Judgment-day

And sat upright. While drearisome
Arose the howl of wakened hounds:
The mouse let fall the altar-crumb,
The worms drew back into the mounds,

The glebe cow drooled. Till God called, 'No;
It's gunnery practice out at sea
Just as before you went below;
The world is as it used to be:

'All nations striving strong to make
Red war yet redder. Mad as hatters
They do no more for Christés sake
Than you who are helpless in such matters.

'That this is not the judgment-hour
For some of them's a blessed thing,
For if it were they'd have to scour
Hell's floor for so much threatening. . . .

'Ha, ha. It will be warmer when
I blow the trumpet (if indeed
I ever do; for you are men,
And rest eternal sorely need).'

So down we lay again. 'I wonder,
Will the world ever saner be',
Said one, 'than when He sent us under
In our indifferent century!'

And many a skeleton shook his head.
'Instead of preaching forty year,'
My neighbour Parson Thirdly said,
'I wish I had stuck to pipes and beer.'

Again the guns disturbed the hour,
Roaring their readiness to avenge,
As far inland as Stourton Tower,
And Camelot, and starlit Stonehenge.

April 1914

Gerard Manley Hopkins *Pied Beauty*

Glory be to God for dappled things –
   For skies of couple-colour as a brinded cow;
     For rose-moles all in stipple upon trout that
        swim;
Fresh-firecoal chestnut-falls; finches' wings;
   Landscape plotted and pieced – fold, fallow, and
        plough;
     And áll trádes, their gear and tackle and trim.
All things counter, original, spare, strange;
   Whatever is fickle, freckled (who knows how?)
     With swift, slow; sweet, sour; adazzle, dim;
He fathers-forth whose beauty is past change:
                  Praise him.

Edward Thomas Tall Nettles

Tall nettles cover up, as they have done
These many springs, the rusty harrow, the plough
Long worn out, and the roller made of stone:
Only the elm butt tops the nettles now.
This corner of the farmyard I like most:
As well as any bloom upon a flower
I like the dust on the nettles, never lost
Except to prove the sweetness of a shower.

The Sun Used to Shine

The sun used to shine while we two walked
Slowly together, paused and started
Again, and sometimes mused, sometimes talked
As either pleased, and cheerfully parted

Each night. We never disagreed
Which gate to rest on. The to be
And the late past we gave small heed.
We turned from men or poetry

To rumours of the war remote
Only till both stood disinclined
For aught but the yellow flavorous coat
Of an apple wasps had undermined:

Or a sentry of dark betonies,
The stateliest of small flowers on earth.
At the forest verge; or crocuses
Pale purple as if they had their birth

In sunless Hades fields. The war
Came back to mind with the moonrise
Which soldiers in the east afar
Beheld then. Nevertheless, our eyes

Could as well imagine the Crusades
Or Cæsar's battles. Everything
To faintness like those rumours fades –
Like the brook's water glittering

Under the moonlight – like those walks
Now – like us two that took them, and
The fallen apples, all the talks
And silences – like memory's sand

When the tide covers it late or soon.
And other men through other flowers
In those fields under the same moon
Go talking and have easy hours.

Digging [1]

Today I think
Only with scents, – scents dead leaves yield,
And bracken, and wild carrot's seed,
And the square mustard field;

Odours that rise
When the spade wounds the root of tree,
Rose, currant, raspberry, or goutweed,
Rhubarb or celery;

The smoke's smell, too,
Flowing from where a bonfire burns
The dead, the waste, the dangerous,
And all to sweetness turns.

It is enough
To smell, to crumble the dark earth,
While the robin sings over again
Sad songs of Autumn mirth.

Aspens

All day and night, save winter, every weather,
Above the inn, the smithy, and the shop,
The aspens at the cross-roads talk together
Of rain, until their last leaves fall from the top.

Out of the blacksmith's cavern comes the ringing
Of hammer, shoe, and anvil; out of the inn
The clink, the hum, the roar, the random singing –
The sounds that for these fifty years have been.

The whisper of the aspens is not drowned,
And over lightless pane and footless road,
Empty as sky, with every other sound
Not ceasing, calls their ghosts from their abode,

A silent smithy, a silent inn, nor fails
In the bare moonlight or the thick-furred gloom,
In tempest or the night of nightingales,
To turn the cross-roads to a ghostly room.

And it would be the same were no house near.
Over all sorts of weather, men, and times,
Aspens must shake their leaves and men may hear
But need not listen, more than to my rhymes.

Whatever wind blows, while they and I have leaves
We cannot other than an aspen be
That ceaselessly, unreasonably grieves,
Or so men think who like a different tree.